Diana Thomson (nee Golding) was born in Manchester on 4th February 1939. She is a sculptor who studied at Kingston Polytechnic (now University) Sculpture Department from 1976–79, obtaining a BA in Fine Art.

Diana was educated at Annisgarth School, Windermere 1946–50 and Cheltenham Ladies' College 1950–55. Shortly after leaving art college, she was commissioned to make several large sculptures, one of which, 'Father and Child', was shown at the Royal Academy Summer Exhibition in 1982. Another is a life-size homage to D.H. Lawrence 1885–1930, sited at Nottingham University. Also, among others, a homage to William Friese-Greene 1855–1921, at four sites: Pinewood Studios, Shepperton Studios, Panavision, Greenford, England and Los Angeles, California, USA.

Married to the Oscar-nominated cinematographer, Alex Thomson, for 44 years, she has one daughter, Chyna.

Diana is now making small pieces of sculpture, and drawing. She is a Fellow of the Royal Society of Sculptors, and an Honorary Friend of the British Society of Cinematographers.

Also by Diana Thomson

A Story for the Children of Today

MY CHAPBOOK
FOR ALEX AND
ALL MY HEROES

A small anthology of poems

BY DIANA THOMSON

SilverWood

Published in 2025 by SilverWood Books

SilverWood Books Ltd
14 Small Street, Bristol, BS1 1DE, United Kingdom
www.silverwoodbooks.co.uk

ISBN 978-1-80042-317-6

British Library Cataloguing in Publication Data
A CIP catalogue record for this book is available from the British Library

Page design and typesetting by SilverWood Books

MY CHAPBOOK
FOR ALEX AND ALL MY HEROES

With thanks to Nicola Rowley

Contents

1   Stirring Februation

With a nod to D.H. Lawrence

Stir up the soil, bring to the boil
Fermenting leaves of yeasty goodness.
Food for the weak, nourishes the bleak
Wartorn, wintrymud, wilderness.

Corpse-ridden beds, plants without heads
Bodies with splendours forgotten.
Owls echo their call, from skeletons tall
Foxes cryhowl for mates yet begotten.

Fortress mole-mound, swords pierce the ground
The battle is on to survive.
As temperatures warm, insects aswarm
A buzzload of bees leave the hive.

Birds high on life, eye up a wife
Count eggs before they are hatched.
Every creature fills, with testosterone thrills
Oh Heaven! We're going to be matched.

Earth Mother moans, Sky father groans
Contriving a huge contraction.
There's no going back, the Force is on track
This life-drive concedes no distraction.

Gaia transforms, nature reforms,
Through meltdown, mayhem and maelstrom.

As new souls arrive, for warm blood they strive
Only God knows where they all come from.

Look! We've come through, as the animals do,
Renaissance refreshed in new skin.
Pleased with our lot, drink a beer, take a tot.
Let The Party of Life begin!

February 2013

2   The Battle of Thixendale

The Battle of Thixendale fought in
Yorkshire and won in Piccadilly,
Heart of England, Capital of Art.

Brave David, armed with sling of paint,
Chosen weapons, Hand, Heart and Eye,
Tempered with generosity and wit,
Scattered sceptics, routed doubters.

"My brush is at the cutting edge, and
Every stroke I make," he swore,
"Will be by my own hand."

Pundits pondered: "How can one man aged
Three score years plus ten, fill twelve
Huge rooms, with paintings all his own?"
This task will take an army. And so it did!

David did not flinch the challenge, and
Summoned up his troops, stout wooden men,
From Rudston Road, Woldgate Woods, joined
Later, by The Bigger Trees Near Warter."

They marched all summer, autumn, winter,
Spring, ablaze with herald-hawthorn-banners,
Proclaiming "Action Week."

Made sorties in broad daylight through
Tunnels lit with snow. Strategies down

Tracks and lanes, over fields and hills,
In trusty jeep with nine all-seeing eyes.

Other allies soon joined in, cohorts of
Cameras, an armoury of i-pad Apple apps.
All help welcomed, embracing modern tools.

Ammunition to conquer the deathly stillness
Of single-point perspective to bring us
Face to face with reality and ever-moving life.

Some troops in Woldgate, felled, did not
Surrender. David brought them back to live
In vivid oranges and blues.

Then triumphant, they gathered up, marched on
To London. Battle won with honesty.
Honour restored with love.

July 2013

Celebration: "David Hockney RA – A Bigger Picture"
Exhibition at The Royal Academy of Arts, London
21st January to 9th April 2012

3 All My Own Work

A seed sown in my gut, you travelled to my heart,
Eventually to be delivered by my hand.
You really were a twinkle in my eye. A spark
In my imagination.

I made a skeleton of steel. Kneaded, pinched and
Shaped your flesh of clay. Searched for the
Form that would define my meaning, in one
Precise mime-gesture.

When you complied, all went well. Sometimes
I wrestled with you. Feared I'd never see
Your birth. Trawled the unknown depths of
My despair, to salvage substance for your life.

Then, silently, miraculously, you emerged from
The sea of doubt. Pristine, complete, my soul
Built into you. A perfect form fulfilling all
Intentions. A mysterious union of heart and hand.

My own creation. And yet not mine.

Like a parent I must let you go, alone into the
World to do your work. Others will assess your
Worth, and what you mean to them. When they
Appraise and look at you, I wonder what they see.
Is it you they recognise or perhaps it could be me?

July 2013

4   Down to Earth

For My Fox

This morning, I was in Iceland. A million
Small geysers rising from the lawn.
A fox was lying in the new hot sun,
Bathing in dew drops and steam.
He lifted his head briefly, looked at me,
And put it down again.
Exhausted from his endless social round
Of picnics, barbecues, festivals and weddings.
In summer he does not need to hunt.
In winter he is never hunted.

He is not pursued by men in hunting pink,
Dressed specially for the chase.
And no-one toasts a stirrup-cup, proclaiming
"Tallyho!"
He has never heard the huntsman's horn, nor
feared the foxhounds' cry.
Dogs bred uniquely for the purpose of his death.
Such pomp and elegance to slay this glamorous
Cad.

No hero he of Ted Hughes 'Thought Fox' fame.
Once muse of poets, painters and artists of
That ilk. His mystique gone, what is he now?
A tramp? A vagrant? Reduced to sorting out
The trash. Irritant of dusty chickens and
Next door's dog. Sometimes he bites a child,

Just to show he's still alive.

No Errol Flynn days and Valentino nights,
Evading his captors with speed and daring.
No-one to throw off-scent, there's no fun
Anymore; in streams, over stones, under
Bridges, crouching in the bracken as the
Hounds race by.
No fat men falling off, or ladies' thrilling
Shrieks.
No challenge to his fiery red-fur cunning or
Silky gauntlet thrown by velvet paw.

To put it bluntly – He is bored.
Self-preservation not his prime concern,
His nature changed, he is defiant, sneering,
Poaching where he can.
He will do anything to pump his heart, to make
Adrenaline.
Excitement is so hard to find, his end I do
Deplore.
It's either call in Pest Control, or be gutted
By a Weybridge 4 X 4.

August 2013

5 Tombs

For D.H. Lawrence and Etruscan Places

I search in tombs carved
One thousand years B.C. to find:

Life
Pale girls and men with swarthy
Sunburnt skin.

I ponder death, three thousand
Years of silence to discover;

Laughter
Music, songs and dance, cavorting
Round the walls.

Fearful, I descend the steep
Dark steps, to confront my

Inheritance:
A legacy of colour, paint traded by
The Greeks, in exchange for Tuscan iron.

La Dolce Vita truly started here,
When Rome was still a hamlet;

Caesarless,
Twelve city states governed wisely
By the Lucumoni

No known language, or preconceived
Ideas, so untroubled by

Professors;
Heaven and Hell, not yet invented.
Another life continues after death.

So wealthy sons and daughters, (girls could
Inherit too)

Venerated
Their creators, with reciprocal creation,
Dwellings for the dead.

Beautiful Necropoli furnished with
Possessions utilised in life.

Quantities
Of vases, bronze, jewels and cloth,
Mirrors and victuals served on priceless
Platters.

All gone now. Looted or sold to
Hungry near-to-death museums.

Etruscans
Let us celebrate, for what is left, is
Something no thief can take; pure joy
And love of life.

Your art. Vital, thrilling, optimistic,
Still throbbing in the womb of its conception.

Eureka!
I have found it. The gift that I have
Waited for. The place of my rebirth.

November 2013

6 Grandma's Christmas

For Albie, Freya and Leila

This is a ditty, it's short and not
Pretty,
From a grumpy old woman of seventy-four
Who's experienced hangovers, sleepovers,
Left-over turnovers, cold Christmas
Turkeys and more.

She's worn out with shopping, cooking and
Mopping.
She's fed up with baking, wrapping and
Stuffing,
Basting and pasting, mincing and slicing,
Roasting and posting; chopping and dicing.
(Not to mention cold-water icing).

She'll kill for a snooze, drink too much
Booze.
Fall over and curse and to make things worse,
Might cook her own goose.

Christmas comes but once a year.
Thank God.
But thank God it will come.

When all's said and done, it's going to
Be fun.
Faces of joy on the girls and the boy.

They get up at dawn, there's snow on the
lawn, Jesus is born.
Walks in the park, lights in the dark,
Smoke in the air, a fireside chair,
Drinks with friends, make amends,
Everyone's there.
I hope we do it again next year.

December 2013

7 Memorials

For My Father,
*   Wing Commander, Albert Golding DFC and Bar*

The naked army marches on.
With its arsenal of stones and chisels,
Paint and paper, brushes, canvas,
Clay and bronze, it travels soundlessly,
Depicting silent images.

How can we interpret the slaughter of
Six million blameless souls, based solely
On their race?
Rachel Whiteread found a way. No words,
But empty books, hidden spines and
Skeletons of stories writ in space.

In Staffordshire, bronze soldier
On stretcher held aloft.
Carved upon adjacent stones, names
Of fifteen thousand lost.
And if this offering does not please
The gods of war,
There is space left for fifteen thousand
More.

Line of painted soldiers, gassed and blind.
His world – a hand placed on any shoulder
He can find.
Shuffling along, not quite dead,

Words his only resource spinning round
His head.

With the help of the poets,
Let us add words to our arms.
No loose cannons, no careless Twitter shot.
Fine stealthy missiles to reveal the
Soldiers' lot.

Words, paint and bronze are no
Substitute for life.
The naked army honours, those who
Really did the work,
And who bravely bore the strife.

January 2014

8 Full Circle

For Stanley Holloway
   (To be read in Lancashire dialect)

"I'll just go t'ut lavatory, then we'll
'ave our tea."
These are shocking words, when you're
Only three.
I don't know if it was 'loo' near the
Same word as 'tea',
That, bemused, confused, and horrified me.

You see, adults obsess what goes in, must
Come out.
If it's in the wrong place, they tend to
Shout.
Lavatory happens after tea.
Who changed them round, I had to see.

I peeped over the sill and took a
Peek,
And there, arse-up, tending her leeks,
Was
MRS ATHERTON.

Under our bedroom was her plot,
And when I looked out, I glimpsed her bot.
What a terrible sight for an innocent
Tot.
MRS ATHERTON!

She, who, to church wore a hat,
She, who, made us stand on the mat,
She, who forbade us to stroke her cat.
She couldn't, she wouldn't, ever say
That.
MRS ATHERTON?

People forget, when you're a child,
That speech is all and should be mild.
We cannot write or even read.
Pictures and words are all we need.
So… the image of Atherton having a wee,
Then sitting directly to have her tea,
Upsets, distresses and still haunts me.

For over seventy years or more,
I feared that Atherton's words were lore.
Up to now I've informed no-one,
But since telling you the trauma has gone.

I can do as I please. I now have a choice.
Liberated, free, from the spooky voice.
But do I?
I'm seventy-five, but might well be three.
Nowadays lavatory is straight after tea.
The familiar order exists today,
And no mistakes, I'm pleased to say.

February 2014

9 When does love become Love?

Love begins at different stages.
Some are born with Love.
Some grow it through their seven ages.
Some come across it suddenly,
Through necessity or trauma.
Some others never get it,
And shrivel in their corner.

The start of it is easy.
When all is young and clean.
Who doesn't love a calf new-born?
A puppy, duckling, soft young fawn?
But this little love, must grow and grow,
To include the old and torn.
When does love become Love?
When we can overcome our scorn.

Life becomes more difficult,
And as we grow love stretches.
It must encompass all mankind,
The charming and the wretches.
We search for it in poetry,
In music and in churches.
When does love become Love?
Is it where the white dove perches?

Perhaps it's in a baby,
Some say it is the sun.
Others swear it is the water,

From which all life must come.
Unique to human beings,
Men and women too.
When does love become Love?
When we can see the other's view.

It could be for Queen and country,
Or President and state.
To help a village neighbour,
A parent or your mate.
Given unconditionally,
Strong, honest, firm yet fair.
When does love become Love?
When bull can live with bear.

May 2014

10 Now and Then

For Memories of a Lancashire Childhood

The streams were crystal clear,
But that was then.
There were frogs aplenty to be caught,
Bread was made and never bought.
But that was then.

Eggs came directly from the hen,
But that was then.
Ginger beer in a tall brown flagon,
Donkeystone, from the ragman's waggon.
But that was then.

Catching carp in the cotton mill pond,
But that was then.
Where even children worked from dawn.
Clogs, clattering in the early morn.
But that was then.

Some things are better, some are worse.
Nostalgia is progression's curse.
But when the traffic roars, I yearn,
To hear the wheels of the milk float turn.
But that was then.

Too much booze, outside loos,
Baths of tin, sex was sin,
Noisy mills, dodgy pills,

Fleas and nits, fetid pits.

I'm glad it's now – not then.

June 2014

11 Boys Will Be Boys

For Dylan Thomas and The Conversation of Prayer

Pink marshmallow light, softens the edges,
Of dark green hedges, where midges fight.
Ferns and grasses, in whispering collusion,
Perform an illusion, in the breeze as it passes.
The fox trots silently patrolling his route.

Shadow shape moved! The boy in the wood,
Froze where he stood. Was it devil cleft-hooved?
Spirits from trees, he had tried to tempt.
It's not what he meant, and he sinks to his knees.
The fox turns briefly and stops in his track.

He held out a charm, to invoke the magic.
A scream almost tragic – stabs the evening calm.
Go back to the tree! What have I done?
It was only for fun. It's not this monster I want to see.
The fox stands and quivers afraid of a trap.

Not sure what he's seen, above a jay mocks,
The boy stares at the fox, then at the mud
where a hole had been.
Down his cheek runs a tear. Was it Satan or Nick?
Its flight was so quick, he is shaking with fear.
The fox curls his lip and snaps at the air.

A dying leaf, a large brown bird.
No sound could be heard, but his chattering teeth

So small and alone. There was a way back,
But the wood looks so black. I want to go home.
The fox is bored and bites his nits.

A bright ray of sun, lights up the wood,
Where the monster had stood, where it started to run.
Immediately clear, that a trick of the light,
Had caused this fright. What a beautiful deer!
The fox sits down and yawns.

Amused by his folly – there was no sin,
Just the fox's grin, he begins to feel jolly.
A triumphant laugh. No need to atone,
He kicks a stone. And then skips down the path.
With a flick of the tail. The fox trots on.

July 2014

12 Me

For Bobby the Cat

Black Knight, Prince of Hunters,
Notching up a kill a day.
Installed upon my lady's bed,
Murderous dreams run round my head.
What trophy shall I bring tonight?
A tortured mouse for her delight.
I raise my tail to catch the favour,
But it's not her gratitude I savour.
Crouching black, I sit alone.
Watching, waiting, preying, praying,
For the faint rustle that uncoils the spring,
That shoots the bolt of death.

NOW!

White bones crunch beneath my jaws.
Crimson squelches through my claws.
Break their legs, so they can't run.
I only do it for the fun.
Tiddles, Pussy, come here Pet.
I haven't brushed your ermine yet.
She coos and cuddles, strokes and fawns.
But I'm the Knight and she, the pawn.
No-one's friend nor cannot be.
For no-one matters more than me.

When I come late, she starts to weep.
Stop that noise and let me sleep.

NOW GO AWAY!

August 2014

13 SOCIAL MEDIA #ilikephiliplarkin

For Philip Larkin
This Be The Verse and An Arundel Tomb

It fucks you up this media fad,
That goes for texting, too.
It gives you friends you never had,
Saying nasty things, untrue.

Great for finding long lost chums.
For images that leave you weak.
People showing off their bums.
It's better dancing cheek to cheek.

Vulgar wordplay makes us laugh,
And go that extra mile.
Puts us on another path,
To insights, offered with a smile.

So take a shot of ether bliss.
Line up, switch on, log in
Where disembodied egos kiss,
Oblivion will win.

In technoheaven you can live,
By feeding from above.
But hearts on earth, are ours to give.
In these survives our love.

November 2014

14 Washing My Face in the Morning

The water runs 'til it feels just right,
The scented soap is soft and light.
The cotton cloth is white and clean.
My face is there; my thoughts unseen.
A reflection mirrors back to me,
Deeds and actions others see.
Was my kindness just invention?
Was it really my intention?
Was I witness to fair play?
Let the others have their say.
This daily ritual is my prayer,
Under worldly dirt another layer.
Hopefully I wash away.
Unworthy deeds of yesterday.
The word describing my ablution,
Is also part of ab(so)lution.

Dec 2014

15 Love at First Light

For the Mountains and Sunsets in Andalucia

I rise from my sleep in the morning.
My smile lights up his craggy face.
I know every wrinkle and crevice,
Every chink, every intimate place.

By noon he tires of my stare,
So I position myself at his shoulder.
His shadow becomes much shorter.
In the afternoon heat I am bolder.

I beam down my whole-hearted love.
Radiate kisses all over his back.
Ignoring me, he is hunched-asleep.
Perhaps I should try a new tack.

So I slip around to his other side,
And head toward my bed.
With diaphanous mauve, I tempt him,
Trailing ribbons of glorious red.

Surprising him, I stroke his neck.
We sink together away from the sea.
I had hoped to move my mountain.
In truth, he moves around me.

February 2015

16 Trespassing

In July sunlight,
Under my teeming tree,
Hung down with hazelnuts,
Suddenly, I spy him.
Shadowy, stick in hand.
Intense, intent.
Focused on his prey,
He does not see me.

Determined, dexterous,
He aims a stick.
And then a stone.
Down descends a deluge.
Golden gifts, wrapped in green.
Given by God and Gaia,
Fruit on trees fair game.
For boys, their natural right.

Surely they belong to me?
But then again, he's having fun.
Smiling to himself,
Jams them up his jumper.
Instinctive, infectious,
I catch his mood,
And decide to join the romp.
"That's right!" I shout.

"Help yourself.
Take as many as you want."

It was as if I struck him.
Startled, shocked, scared,
My generosity ill-timed,
He drops the lot and runs away.
"Come back," I call. But he
Bolts. Not even looking back.

Then – it strikes – me.
The nuts were just a target. He,
Practising primeval survival skill,
Was jolted from his ancient world,
Where I had trespassed. And
something, some connection,
To my mundane adult life,
Was lost forever.

May 2015

17 In Praise of Cadmium (Cd 48)

For Vincent van Gogh and Paul Cezanne

In subterranean depths where Orcus rules,
Dragons belch flames to feed the forge,
Vulcan's furnace fires earth's crust to make
Manna for the artist.

Not stirred in heaven,
But in hot hell, the volcanic feast erupts
Through tiny tubes of lead.
There is no danger,
For the painter's sable sword, weapon of
Pacific choice, transfers this vibrant food onto
The white cloth.

Before us, apples, pears,
Oranges, a jug of wine set out,
palatable,
Only for the eyes.

So, through your gaze,
Feed the spirit and tell the gods of Dis, that their
Work is transported to the upper realms,
From the periodic table to the canvas table, by the
Divine Creator at work within the human brain.

June 2015

www.ingramcontent.com/pod-product-compliance
Lightning Source LLC
Chambersburg PA
CBHW030637150426
42813CB00050B/66